Book 1

Nonfiction

I Can Pat

Not everything should be touched. Learn about some things you can and cannot pat.

Phonics Focus: *Short a*

Words to Learn

This book contains homophones, or words that are spelled the same, but have different meanings. Encourage your child to explore the multiple meanings of *bat* and *jam*.

Phonics Focus Words		High-Frequency Words	
bat	jam	a	not
can	pan	I	this
cat	pat		
hat	tap		

Before Reading

Ask your child what it means to pat (to touch something lightly). Have them brainstorm a list of things they know they can and cannot pat. Ask your child to flip through the pages and look at the photographs. Encourage them to share what they notice about the pictures. Ask your child to look at the cover of the book. Have them share what they notice. Ask them what they think they will read about in this book.

Explain the **Phonics Focus** of the book and go over any **Words to Learn**. Tell your child that in this book they will read many words that have the *short a* sound. Have your child say the sound: /ă/. Use the words from the title as examples. The words *can* and *pat* both have the *short a* sound.

During Reading

Have your child check their predictions as they read. Allow them to connect to the text and photographs through their own experiences. Encourage your child to ask questions while they read to learn, infer, and draw conclusions.

Ask your child to focus on the words that have the *short a* sound. Have them point out words on the pages that have this sound. Prompt them to think about other words they know that have the *short a* sound.

After Reading

Ask your child to go back and check their predictions. *What did they get right? What was different from what they expected? What did they learn?* Have your child turn to specific pages they want to share about. Ask them to recall details using questioning. *What is something you can pat? What was the difference between the cat you can pat and the cat you cannot pat?* Ask your child to share what they would add to the book as something they can pat and something they cannot pat.

Book 2

Fiction

We Will Win!

Kit and Pip have a contest to see who can hit the bin with their empty juice boxes.

Phonics Focus: *Short i*

Words to Learn

This book uses the word *rig*. Explain that *rig* means to make or set up something quickly and with what you have on hand. In the word *miss*, the ending letters make one /s/ sound.

Phonics Focus Words		Decodable Words		High-Frequency Words	
big	Pip	am	can	and	the
bin	rig			I	we
did	sip				
fix	sit				
hit	will				
in	win				
it	zig				
Kit	zip				
miss					

Before Reading

Ask your child what it means to work together. Have them think of a time they needed to work together to do something. Encourage them to share their answers. Ask your child to flip through the pages and look at the illustrations. Encourage them to share what they notice about the pictures. Ask your child to look at the cover of the book. Have them share what they notice. Ask them what they think they will read about in this book.

Explain the **Phonics Focus** of the book and go over any **Words to Learn**. Tell your child that in this book they will read many words that have the *short i* sound. Have your child say the sound: /ĭ/. Use the words from the title as examples. The words *will* and *win* both have the *short i* sound.

During Reading

Have your child check their predictions as they read. Allow them to connect to the text and illustrations through their own experiences. Encourage your child to ask questions while they read to learn, infer, and draw conclusions.

Ask your child to focus on the words that have the *short i* sound. Have them point out words on the pages that have this sound. Prompt them to think about other words they know that have the *short i* sound.

After Reading

Ask your child to go back and check their predictions. *What did they get right? What was different from what they expected? What did they learn?* Have your child turn to specific pages they want to share about. Ask them to recall details using questioning. *Who is Pip? Why did Kit think she would win? How did Kit and Pip get the juice box into the bin?* Ask your child who their favorite character was from the book, Kit or Pip. Then, ask them to explain why.

Book 3

Nonfiction

Lots of Dogs

Dogs come in all shapes and sizes. They can be pets and have jobs. Learn about some dogs in this book.

Phonics Focus: *Short o*

Words to Learn

In the words *lots* and *dots*, the *s* at the ends of the words makes the /s/ sound. In the word *dogs*, the *s* at the end of the word makes the /z/ sound.

Phonics Focus Words		Decodable Words		High-Frequency Words	
Bot	lot(s)	big	Fab	a	of
box	not	Bit	Jak	has	this
dog(s)	on			is	
Don	Oz				
dot(s)	pop				
fox	Rob				
hog	Tod				
job	top				

Before Reading

Ask your child to tell about their dog, a dog they would like to have, or a dog a friend or family member has. Allow your child time to share the dog's name, appearance, and other details. Ask your child to flip through the pages and look at the photographs. Encourage them to share what they notice about the pictures. Ask your child to look at the cover of the book. Have them share what they notice. Ask them what they think they will read about in this book.

Explain the **Phonics Focus** of the book and go over any **Words to Learn**. Tell your child that in this book they will read many words that have the *short o* sound. Have your child say the sound: /ŏ/. Use the singular forms of words from the title as examples. The words *lot* and *dog* both have the *short o* sound.

During Reading

Have your child check their predictions as they read. Allow them to connect to the text and photographs through their own experiences. Encourage your child to ask questions while they read to learn, infer, and draw conclusions.

Ask your child to focus on the words that have the *short o* sound. Have them point out words on the pages that have this sound. Prompt them to think about other words they know that have the *short o* sound.

After Reading

Ask your child to go back and check their predictions. *What did they get right? What was different from what they expected? What did they learn?* Have your child turn to specific pages they want to share about. Ask them to recall details using questioning. *Which dog has dots? Who is a big dog? Who is not big? Which dog has a job?* Ask your child who their favorite dog was from the book and why.

Book 4

Fiction

Gum Is Fun!

Gum can be fun . . . and messy! Bud and his dog Pug have fun with gum until Mom tells them to clean up!

Phonics Focus: *Short u*

Words to Learn

In the word *yuck*, the *c* and *k* together make the /k/ sound.

Phonics Focus Words		Decodable Words		High-Frequency Words	
Bud	rug	got	on	a	is
bus	run	in	pop	and	the
fun	tub	mom		has	
gum	tug				
hug	yuck				
Pug	yum				
rub					

Before Reading

Ask your child if they have ever chewed a piece of gum. Ask them what they can do with gum such as stretch it or blow bubbles. Ask them to think about how gum feels. Let your child share their experiences with gum. Ask your child to flip through the pages and look at the illustrations. Encourage them to share what they notice about the pictures. Ask your child to look at the cover of the book. Have them share what they notice. Ask them what they think they will read about in this book.

Explain the **Phonics Focus** of the book and go over any **Words to Learn**. Tell your child that in this book they will read many words that have the *short u* sound. Have your child say the sound: /ŭ/. Use the words from the title as examples. The words *gum* and *fun* both have the *short u* sound.

During Reading

Have your child check their predictions as they read. Allow them to connect to the text and illustrations through their own experiences. Encourage your child to ask questions while they read to learn, infer, and draw conclusions.

Ask your child to focus on the words that have the *short u* sound. Have them point out words on the pages that have this sound. Prompt them to think about other words they know that have the *short u* sound.

After Reading

Ask your child to go back and check their predictions. *What did they get right? What was different from what they expected? What did they learn?* Have your child turn to specific pages they want to share about. Ask them to recall details using questioning. *What is one thing Bud gets gum on? What gets on the rug? How does the mom feel at the end of the story?* Ask your child to share what they would do if they got gum on something.

Book 5

Nonfiction

An Egg for Meg

Meg's hen has eggs. Read this book to learn what Meg does with one of the eggs.

Phonics Focus: *Short e*

Words to Learn
In the word *eggs*, the *s* at the end of the word makes the /z/ sound.

Phonics Focus Words		Decodable Words		High-Frequency Words	
egg(s)	Meg	an	hot	a	the
get	set	cup	in	for	
hen	ten	got	pot		
let		had			

Before Reading

Engage your child in a discussion about eggs. *Do they know where eggs come from? What are different ways eggs can be cooked?* Brainstorm a list of different ways to cook eggs. Ask your child to flip through the pages and look at the photographs. Encourage them to share what they notice about the pictures. Ask your child to look at the cover of the book. Have them share what they notice. Ask them what they think they will read about in this book.

Explain the **Phonics Focus** of the book and go over any **Words to Learn**. Tell your child that in this book they will read many words that have the *short e* sound. Have your child say the sound: /ĕ/. Use the words from the title as examples. The words *egg* and *Meg* both have the *short e* sound.

During Reading

Have your child check their predictions as they read. Allow them to connect to the text and photographs through their own experiences. Encourage your child to ask questions while they read to learn, infer, and draw conclusions.

Ask your child to focus on the words that have the *short e* sound. Have them point out words on the page that have this sound. Prompt them to think about other words they know that have the *short e* sound.

After Reading

Ask your child to go back and check their predictions. *What did they get right? What was different from what they expected? What did they learn?* Have your child turn to specific pages they want to share about. Ask them to recall details using questioning. *What animal does the egg come from? How many eggs did Meg take? What did Meg do with the egg before she ate it?* Ask your child to tell what breakfast they like to eat. *Does it have eggs?*

Book 6

Fiction

Chad and Chen

Learn all about how Chad and Chen have fun together in this book about friendship.

Phonics Focus: *Digraph ch*

Words to Learn

This book uses the word *chum* as a synonym for the word *friend*. Discuss the meaning of the word *chum* and explain that synonyms are words that have similar meanings and can often be used interchangeably.

Phonics Focus Words		Decodable Words		High-Frequency Words	
Chad	chop	an	had	a	her
chat	chum	big	it	and	was
Chen	inch	dot	on		
chin	such	fun			
chip					

Before Reading

Talk with your child about friendship. *What makes someone a good friend?* Ask your child to flip through the pages and look at the illustrations. Encourage them to share what they notice about the pictures. Ask your child to look at the cover of the book. Have them share what they notice. Ask them what they think they will read about in this book.

Explain the **Phonics Focus** of the book and go over any **Words to Learn**. Tell your child that in this book they will read many words that have the *ch digraph*. The letters *c* and *h* together make a new sound. Have your child say the sound: /ch/. Use the words from the title as examples. The words *Chad* and *Chen* both have the *ch digraph*.

During Reading

Have your child check their predictions as they read. Allow them to connect to the text and illustrations through their own experiences. Encourage your child to ask questions while they read to learn, infer, and draw conclusions.

Ask your child to focus on the words that have the *ch digraph*. Have them point out words on the page that have this sound. Prompt them to think about other words they know that have the *ch digraph*.

After Reading

Ask your child to go back and check their predictions. *What did they get right? What was different from what they expected? What did they learn?* Have your child turn to specific pages they want to share about. Ask your child to recall details using questioning. *What food did both Chad and Chen have? What sport do Chad and Chen like? What word in the book means "friend"?* Ask your child to tell about someone who is a good friend.

Book 7

Nonfiction

At the Pet Shop

A child visits a pet shop and wishes to get a pet. Learn all about what she gets.

Phonics Focus: *Digraph sh*

Words to Learn

This book uses the word *dash*. Discuss the different meanings of the word. Explain that *dash* in this story means *a small amount*.

Phonics Focus Words		Decodable Words		High-Frequency Words	
cash	rush	at	on	a	I
dash	ship	fed	pet	are	the
dish	shop	get	sat	for	to
fish	wish	in	set	has	with
mesh		Mom	top		
		net			

Before Reading

Ask your child to share what they know about pet shops. *What can people buy at a pet shop?* Ask your child to flip through the pages and look at the photographs. Encourage them to share what they notice about the pictures. Ask your child to look at the cover of the book. Have them share what they notice. Ask them what they think they will read about in this book.

Explain the **Phonics Focus** of the book and go over any **Words to Learn.** Tell your child that in this book they will read many words that have the *sh digraph.* Have your child say the sound: /sh/. Use a word from the title as an example. The word *shop* has the *sh digraph.*

During Reading

Have your child check their predictions as they read. Allow them to connect to the text and photographs through their own experiences. Encourage your child to ask questions while they read to learn, infer, and draw conclusions.

Ask your child to focus on the words that have the *sh digraph.* Have them point out words on the page that have this sound. Prompt them to think about other words they know that have the *sh digraph.*

After Reading

Ask your child to go back and check their predictions. *What did they get right? What was different from what they expected? What did they learn?* Have your child turn to specific pages they want to share about. Ask them to recall details using questioning. *What does the child wish for at the shop? What does her mom use to buy a fish? What does she put a fish in?* Ask your child to imagine they are getting a fish. *What will it look like? What is its name?*

Book 8

Fiction

The Long Sock

Duck shows off to Chick what he can do with a long sock. Find out whose sock it is.

Phonics Focus: *Digraphs ng and ck*

Words to Learn

This book contains two tricky words that end with the *long i* sound, but are spelled differently. The word *hi* ends with an *i* that says its own name: /ī/. The word *my* ends with a *y* that says /ī/.

Phonics Focus Words		Decodable Words		High-Frequency Words	
Chick	long	can	on	a	my
ding	neck	in	such	hi	put
dong	rock	it		I	that
Duck	sock			is	
hang	wing				

Before Reading

Ask your child what it means to respect other people's property. *Should you take something that does not belong to you? How would you feel if someone took something of yours?* Ask your child to flip through the pages and look at the illustrations. Encourage them to share what they notice about the pictures. Ask your child to look at the cover of the book. Have them share what they notice. Ask them what they think they will read about in this book.

Explain the **Phonics Focus** of the book and go over any **Words to Learn**. Tell your child that in this book they will read many words that have the *ng* or *ck digraph*. Have them say the sounds: /ng/ and /k/. Use the words from the title as examples. The word *long* has the *ng digraph* and the word *sock* has the *ck digraph*.

During Reading

Have your child check their predictions as they read. Allow them to connect to the text and illustrations through their own experiences. Encourage your child to ask questions while they read to learn, infer, and draw conclusions.

Ask your child to focus on the words that have the *ng* or *ck digraph*. Have them point out words on the page that have these sounds. Prompt them to think about other words they know that have the *ng* or *ck digraph*.

After Reading

Ask your child to go back and check their predictions. *What did they get right? What was different from what they expected? What did they learn?* Have your child turn to specific pages they want to share about. Ask them to recall details using questioning. *What did Duck wrap the sock around? Where did Duck hang the sock? What did Chick think of the sock?* Ask your child to share something of theirs that is very special. *What makes it so special? How would you feel if you lost it?*